Mr. Duvall Reports the News

written by
JILL D. DUVALL

photographs by
LILI DUVALL

Reading Consultant
LINDA CORNWELL
Learning Resource Consultant
Indiana Department of Education

CHILDREN'S PRESS® *A Division of Grolier Publishing*
New York • London • Hong Kong • Sydney • Danbury, Connecticut

Dedicated to Gracie, Rachel, Natalie, and Donovan

Special thanks to David Hopper, Gus Gomez, Jed's coworkers, and makeup artist Amy Sue Mechalek

Library of Congress Cataloging-in-Publication Data
Duvall, Jill.
    Mr. Duvall reports the news / written by Jill D. Duvall ; photographs by Lili Duvall.
       p.   cm. — (Our neighborhood)
    Summary: Follows a television correspondent from fact-finding to broadcast as he reports important news to his community.
    ISBN 0-516-20316-9 (lib. bdg.)— ISBN 0-516-26150-9 (pbk.)
    1. Duvall, Jed. 2. Journalists—United States—Biography—Juvenile literature. 3. Television broadcasting of news—United States—Juvenile literature. [1. Journalists. 2. Occupations. 3. Television broadcasting of news.] I. Duvall, Lili, ill. II. Title. III. Series: Our neighborhood.
    PN4874.D88D885   1997
    070′.92—dc20
    [B]   96-34915
                                          CIP
                                          AC

Photographs ©: Jim Greene: 6; Aaron Sasson: 7; all other photos: Lili Duvall.

Mr. Jed Duvall reports the news on television. News stories are facts about people who live in a community.

Mr. Duvall checks to see what his next story will be. Before he can tell a news story, he must get the information.

Mr. Duvall travels to places all over the world. In Pennsylvania, he reported news about a flood.

In Israel and Egypt, he gathered facts to tell to people in America.

When Mr. Duvall travels, he always brings his computer.

Wherever he is, Mr. Duvall hears many speeches.

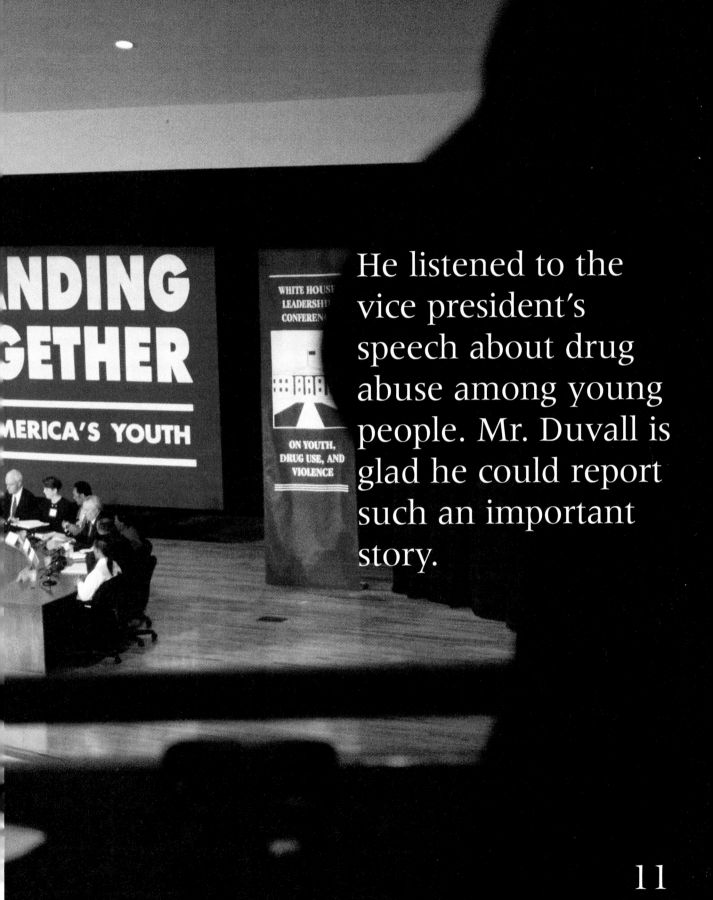

He listened to the vice president's speech about drug abuse among young people. Mr. Duvall is glad he could report such an important story.

Before a news story can be on
television, many people must
work together.

Some people
shoot the pictures.

Once the pictures are on tape,
another person shows Mr. Duvall
the best pictures to use.

Mr. Duvall compares his notes with the producer's to make sure he has all the right facts.

Now it's time for Mr. Duvall to write the script to his story.

This is the part of the job he likes best, because he can share what he knows with other people.

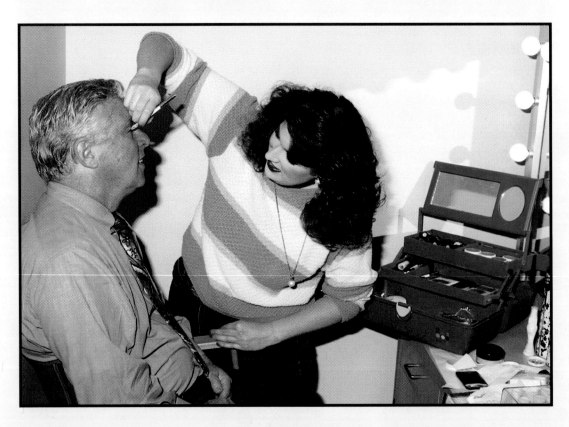

But he doesn't like wearing makeup! He needs to wear it only when he reports from a television news studio.

The television news studio has so many buttons and dials! The director watches Mr. Duvall get ready to report his story.

Mr. Duvall wears an earpiece so he can hear the director.

He wears a tiny microphone so we can hear what he says.

Mr. Duvall looks like he is talking right to us, but he is really talking to a camera.

He reads the story from a machine called a "TelePrompTer."

Off to another story! Mr. Duvall
must show his press pass to the
guard at the White House.

Stories about the president of the United States are very important to our community.

Mr. Duvall doesn't know where he will be going next, but he is always ready to bring us another exciting news story.

Meet the Photographer and the Author

Lili Duvall decided when she was in her teens that she wanted to take pictures. She is now a professional photographer and taking pictures of children is her favorite work. Her home and studio are in Maryland.

Jill Duvall, Lili's writing partner, is also her mother. And Jed Duvall, the subject of this book, is Lili's father. Jill likes living near Washington, D.C., because much of her studying and writing is about the government. Jill feels that writing is very important and even takes her writing to the beach!